Janet's Cottage

Janet's Cottage

POEMS

D. H. Tracy

WINNER OF THE NEW CRITERION POETRY PRIZE

St. Augustine's Press
SOUTH BEND, IN 2012

Funding for this year's New Criterion Poetry Prize
has been provided by Joy & Michael Millette

www.staugustine.net

Library of Congress Cataloging-in-Publication Data:

Tracy, D. H.
    Janet's cottage: poems / D. H. Tracy
        p. cm
    "Winner of the New Criterion Poetry Prize."
    ISBN 978-1-58731-393-6 (alk. paper)
    I. Title.
    PS3620.R3287J36 2011
    811'.6—dc23   2011036803

∞The paper used in this publication meets the minimum requirements of the American Nation
Standard for Information Sciences—Permanence of Paper for Printed Materials, ANSI Z39.48-198

Contents

IV

Acknowledgments

Grateful acknowledgment is made to the following publications in which some of the poems in this book have previously appeared: *32 Poems*, "Tenth Flight"; *American Poetry Review*, "Vanitas: Globe"; *Blue Mesa Review*, "Norwalk's 350th"; *Crab Orchard Review*, "Carmon's," "Sketches of J."; *The Iowa Review*, "Utopia Sketched"; *Literary Imagination*, "Vanitas: Bells"; *Michigan Quarterly Review*, "Miss Lucy, *cont'd*"; *Mid-American Review*, "Of the Model Boaters"; *New Delta Review*, "On Janis Joplin and William Bennett's Blind Date, 1969"; *Passages North*, "Safiya's Recife Diary"; *Poetry*, "One Connecticut," "Lapse of Faculty," "The Explorer at Eureka Dunes," "Catastrophe"; *Potomac Review*, "Cliché Parade"; *Prairie Schooner*, "Lines on the West Resist Translation," "To England"; *Smartish Pace*, "Janet's Cottage"; *TriQuarterly*, "The Neighbor Discusses Parkinson's," "Clutch"; *The Yale Review*, "AWOL." "Vanitas: Bells" was written in the course of a bookmaking collaboration with the artist Jill Grimes.

Janet's Cottage

I

Vanitas: Bells

Loud even on the quarter hour they
  sound the public on-passing
for those ears not removed too far upwind,
and the blow they deal leaves a bruise lasting
  the listener on his way
longer than they will take to strike again.

Full of want, the bell wants what its toller
  tells it to want, so its tongue
wags madly in its mouth, craving, and leaves
the diffident fiat that it sang
  trailing off, until its sole
point is the suppression of our speech.

Incursion, wedding, sabbath, fire, and time
  that we have made occasion
the cast bronze quiet almost always,
while in the thickets the heraldings dun
  the dove- and chaparral-mind:
the bell may tell apart these causes.

On the mountainside, a manzanita leaf
  may enfold a squirrel skull,
and the campanile in the distance
may not be ringing; and the air is full
  of that which bells break: of grief,
and the quartering harriers' patience.

In the field glass appears the caravan
   of the dead, dusted skeletons
in turbans and Tudor hats washing their feet
in the stream; as the stream runs through their hands,
   so breath through them and their pavane
of drum and fiddle, chime and castanet.

The Explorer at Eureka Dunes

Found them. Sand enough to levee the Amazon.
Make buckshot of pearls. Then rustle awhile
in forever's hourglass. So fragile
they calve under the rat-treads dusted on

before daybreak. But sterner than the rock they used to be.
Able to handle the climate better.
Geologically hell-for-leather
the great aisles shiver downwind. In their lee

dunegrass and primrose, unaccountable. Some will want
accounting anyway. Pressings. A sketch
of each. Conjectures of what the milkvetch
does in other seasons. The transit and the sextant,

my plain-dealing emissaries, will not fix them.
I'll lay them back in their cases, neat,
having put the height at seven hundred feet.
That figure—wrong already, growing wronger, fiction—

will not credit much the received portrait. My report's failure
does leave the local strangeness intact;
I will have folded away its fact
into my spare and private republic. Therein a danger

maybe worse. Imagination wants them free,
higher, brighter, would have them prove
that reverie will not remove
them from themselves. I have no general dunes in me,

only those seen on the visit. If a child
should want to hear a desert tale,
the being-there might not avail
the teller. The being-there might not avail the told.

One Connecticut

The dinosaur prints cannot calibrate their novelty.
Reservoir three inches low.
Thirty miles as a rule
to a place that is not Connecticut.
Blockish land of supposed propriety!
A Greek girl I really loved has moved to Iowa.
Hell: history, geology.
The nutmegs in the stories grew
in the tropics. Bully for glaciers.
The maple branches fashion
a brittle arbor too seldom lush.
Somehow the devices held together.
Lawnmowers. Stage lights
at the high school. Vaccines that forestalled
I know not what.
Connecticut lays itself at the feet of my hatred.
The accent the Ischians use when not among themselves
does not point to but is Connecticut.
Red by oak. Blue by May. White by sailcloth
jacketed on the booms in the marinas.
As it does not go on forever
Connecticut warrants heated response.
Moderate rivers blacken the spillways,
and the labels of the green and dun bottles
are affixed in an album withheld from me.
Swan. Nuthatch. Birdwatcher.
Connecticut may be notional.

Fourth week in August, by the train tracks,
sumac growing in crack in asphalt
extends branch through chain-link fence.
White shingles / black shutters, stone wall.
The helicopter factory.
Consideration of blood will lend our spirits weight
in the absence of a satisfactory founding myth.
The gutshot cities sag.
The ponds crack like china. I have
passed my days in the dread of errands.

Vanitas: Globe

Like a spitted, shrunken head the cardboard earth
rotates backwards on two squeaking bearings,
   wobbling in a reticle
of parallels and elemental pairings,
   like land and sea, and north and south,
the compass and the monster's tentacle.

A mockup made consistent with the news
of everyone fanned out to grasp its shape,
   the globe is in and of its time,
was never intended to anticipate
   the changes in our premises
or outlast questions urgent in its prime;

or has eternity endorsed the globe,
and given to its sphere an atmosphere
   of constant worldwide light of noon
to tell us that the last and actual here
   is too-bad for the claustrophobe
and what we can expect of sun and moon?

In a city not on the globe they contrive
geodesic globes of glue and matchsticks
   and a globe so big one can enter it
and comment whisperingly on the strange acoustics—
   while hollering festival-goers give
balls of marzipan and chocolate

from egg-piñatas in the bungo trees,
and fishnetted glass-globes in the windows strain
 colors consumed in a place inside them
the private tolerance of bliss and pain
 knows by the vivid pleasantries
allowed into the air to hide them.

The Judge Answers the Sorcerer

after Shehe Muhiuddini

Python! A waste of thought,
weighing your devilry
against the run of thieves'
I gather that the fees
charged for your artistry
will turn a have to have-not,

yet leave live men cowed
by otherworldly shills.
Heron-spirits, drum-wraiths
must know the weakest faiths
dwell in the weakest wills.
Which one of them allowed

Halifan out to stroll
Kokoni as we speak?
It is as if your "ghost
of drunkenness" had lost
interest, proved meek,
and returned to him his soul.

The crowd awaits its answer—
or, let them reckon the odds
my words are magic which
your magic feathered switch

and what, divining rods,
will banish altogether.

Or are you off to forage
for the forest's rarest berry,
and make of it the potions
sold door to door to matrons,
where, I'm told, you tarry,
sampling their porridge?

In public he admits
to no ambition, yet,
like Haman at his tower,
in private, covets power,
and would have us in his debt:
a Pharaoh of the fits.

Has he robbed your tongues?
With every word unsaid
you shirk your labor, sheep.
Better you were asleep
than full waking and misled.
By what would you know kings,

if you cannot see the faithless?
An apostate has his tale,
but you, your creed misplaced,
lend credence to disgrace,
and revel in the sale.
Possessed—yes—by darkness.

AWOL

Our slitted eyes accost him, where and when
we have nothing better to do than make
a sacrament of our own industry.
At bus stops and in line. Our chiding eyes
have become his element to weather,
a condition. Other times, we only watch,
from shop windows, the concrete sanding down
his sneaker soles, or glimpse him
wading the medians and culvert grass,
thumb not out. The young deserve discomfort,

which is why we put him in the navy.
We have changed, though, his linens at the hostel,
washed the ashes off and patched the burn-holes,
and fingered the ragged edges of the envelopes
kept in his pillowcase. We picked off the floor
his matinee stub bookmark. We also have been
the too-skeptical bunkmate, and tales
of jumping ship have rung, not false, abstract.
Abstract. Magazines lie in his lap,
absorbing him. The wayward deserve

correction, but ostracism will not work
in his case. We have tried to bring him in,
giving him free refills, and throwing him
a flirtatious word to liven his campouts
in the corner booth, and remind him

what he has given up. His gaze extends
out the filmed windows, down to the harbor;
he eyes the great gray eminences,
the aircraft sulking on the decks, the white-
liveried hands, deserving, he might think,

to be torpedoed to fuck-all. We have made him
look the miscreant without trying to do so,
though we have tried to do so. He has paid
with nickels and dimes for cigarettes, and lingered
at the station counter turning out his pockets.
We have begrudged him twenty, fifteen,
ten more cents, and pressed into his hand
the several small victories of ease
he will win among us. The streetlights
lay down their capes for him. The willful

deserve comeuppance, or envy of their will
would rule us. Then there might be no place to take
leave of. He has set his elbows on the railing
of the bridge. He has very slowly chalked his cue.
He has pulled a cap around his ears and left,
but is never absent. He has scorned
our elected futures, that seem to him
hobbled for the choosing. We have set
the outlawry. We have muted awe
of his taste for panic. He has not said uncle.

Of the Model Boaters

Life-size sailors on life-size seas have lent them
the awkwardness of wind awhile to manage,
and the model boaters turn their hands to this
as if to a repair, or to resolve
the business matter of an ailing friend.
They hush in an exertion of pretend
while the white handkerchiefs of sail go scudding
atop radio-controlled cockleshells,
surrendering the grownup offices.
The boaters leave their uniforms at home,
whether banker's, baker's, or cabinetmaker's;
there is no talk of money, no crumbs or sawdust,
no vestige of the trances in their havens
set so thoroughly aside it seems
a mutiny was organized and staged,
in the fullness of their concentration,
on and of their concentration. No one
does them the favor they do. Will you
set your life aside and go to them,
envy them with all your powers the length
of one September afternoon? To toast
their adventitious goodness would not go
as far as having made a model boat.
Could you match them, and make a model doughnut
or fuss with sheaves of foreign currency
until your origami trees were fruiting
origami coins? Would you fill

your lottery tickets with the digits from
their passing little penciled calculations?
Underneath the model boats the murk
of nausea and music, rivalries,
the undistinguished rhythms of the day. . . .
What congratulation can one mouth
not lost on this contempt-elided zone
of residence and business? Talk and you
will find you have become more feckless than
a model boater. Somewhere men lay out
cream papers, uncap a fountain pen, and wait
for you to come around to folly, sign,
be handed keys to the quiet garret, sit
at its pitted desk and watch the rooftops age.
There is a civil service sinecure.
There is a view of the canal. You might
look after yourself awhile, or give some thought
to death and suffering and beauty; you are,
they say, a prestigious being after all.
That sullen and minor something somehow gotten
in the sailing of a model boat, not gotten
in captaining—never to know its nature,
even as the washed-up sailors gather
at the canal these splendid days, and guard
our disappearing pangs of jealousy.

II

Norwalk's 350th

Atlantic regalia commandeered
from sponsors and municipal garages
files up West Ave., aimed, though weird,
at splendor something like the Raj's.

So send one up for the Girl Scouts
and cheer the department of public works.
Columbus, too, though on the outs
with history, still enjoying perks.

The high school band, whose color guard
with lots of makeup cops the look
of somewhere organized and hard,
plays "On Wisconsin," and a truck

kerchiefed in a Puerto Rican
banner grinds down gears to keep
from overrunning the American
Legionnaires. A vintage jeep

darts around the vintage tank,
flashing a shot-up road sign stenciled
Paris 15k. Honk-honk.
Fifteen, you wish. The GIs' guild

still marches, game; fallen in behind,
the increasingly nimble comers-back

onlookers jumble in the mind—
Korea, Vietnam, Iraq?

—and ROTC in step presenting
arms like May Day Soviets,
from the same planet as our agitating
bob-cut flapper suffragettes.

O frock'd Hungarians! Connecticut Sikhs!
Orthodox Greeks and prim Rotarians!
Any way you slice it freaks,
worthies, *menschen*, and barbarians.

Retired engines in period plumage
command a berth. The no-alarm event
splats against the harbor frontage,
a hose of pageantry left to vent

point-three-odd millennia of occupation.
My stars, we've made it—tentativer
than others in its celebration,
but showing—no?—that *savoir vivre*:

twelve-year-olds in three-cornered hats
who fife and snare the Union hymn.
Don't tread on me. Simple as that?
Nor tread on her; nor tread on him.

Safiya's Recife Diary

Peeking into the mosques back in Sanaa
I watched the bleached rows rise together
and fall until Salim gave us away
with his foolish mouth. Just then there was no question.
I would live forever beside that spotless machine,
asking its permission for everything—
while smiles came out some times and grumpy men
to swat at our backsides others. Imagine.
So different, Brazilians! They have no place
to keep you out of. None to be let into either.
They resemble too much the plaza's pigeons, alike
in every way but color, pecking food
out of their neighbors' mouths. Each for himself.
Shameful. Lucky the scooter never comes
to shoo them. When it does they all
take flight at once, and sometimes for an eye-blink I see them
make a tent they are all inside of.
                              It must have been
restlessness, halfway through their lives like that,
or the silver business going down the tube, or taxes
going up. Something was eating them. Me
not old enough to flirt and my mother still
with her *Stay away from these Hadhramauti Sunnite whoresons*
once a month, once a week, once a day. Evenings
after she fed Dad she cooed *Salam,*
Israel in his ear and it made him grimace
like she had stuck a drill in his tooth, *zoop,*

like that. And he said *You know as well as I do*
that genius magic carpet—and they both sagged
to think of their parents' forgotten village and to this
Mom could not reply. But one night the map came out.
I remember on one corner my father's pliers,
teacups on two others, Salim filthy
on the fourth. Dad said, *Where?* Mom squeezed my shoulders.
I pointed to California. Salim left his thumbprint
on Durban. And Dad grunted as he did
to give assent to something he knew did not
need it, clapped, split the difference, and said,
Brazil.

      The journey, who cares. I see this now.
You arrive if you arrive. If bandits clobber you
or whales eat you no one will never know
to miss you. But then we still thought we were
important—when Mom saw the boat in Aden
she said *I would not sail this up the falaj*
and prayed the whole way out of the harbor. Dad
looked back on the mountains that meant who-knows-what
to him, and I watched his knuckles go white
around the railing and his face go red,
a little. One of the Filipinos with the crew
knew Arabic—Bahraini accent, up that side—
and I asked him many questions through Salim.
Had he been to Brazil? He had. Had he liked it?
Indeed, yes. He was old, older than my father,
missing his lower front teeth. A tattoo of a rooster
on his forearm. What do they think of Yemenis?
At this he laughed quietly, for a long time,
then patted our shoulders and went off to work,
and he is the last person I remember knowing
before the land came into view and with it

this city too helter-skelter for its visitors
to irritate, and we became small again.

                                  Before
we met in school I had seen Mateus sometimes
on the corner not far from the apartment, handing
pamphlets out like a maniac. When I walked by
he yelled *Save the rain forest!* like I, Safiya,
am responsible. I have never even seen the place.
Rain forest, what. I ignored him. The next week
at school he introduced himself. At first
I was very embarrassed but with his lectures
on *deforestation* and *land-use reform* there is
no quiet for awkwardness the whole way home.
Salim told on me, of course, and my mother's
Hadhramauti whoresons having become
worthless Pernambucan pigs there was
explaining to do. *Where is he from?* Recife.
But—what is his family name? Hofstadter.
Dad sat down with a thud. Mom crossed herself
in this habit she has picked up from the Brazilian women.
I am not worried. After the day at his workshop
my father comes home not to the small apartment
but to the quiet mansion of his own sadness—
and yet I have seen him on the phone with cousins
who tease him for coming to Brazil, and he holds
one hand in the air like screwing in a light bulb,
a gesture of triumph they cannot see, and he says
the first synagogue in the Americas! He hums
bossa nova in the shower and he discusses
the Falkland Islands with the neighbors. I tell him
this was in Argentina. He says
It is a matter of regional interest. My mother
rides the bus crosstown for an Arab grocery

and I have caught her drinking tea with the lady
who works there who is a Muslim. All of us
act loopier than we did.
                    I know M.
is not serious. He asks me to come to the beach
with his friends and to wear a bikini. I tell him
it's all I can do to go out without a scarf.
He says *Sister it's not your head I want*
uncovered so I know he is not serious.
But I wonder sometimes what our child might look like.
It is strange. No face comes to mind. Then
sometimes out walking I see a little girl
and think, Our child will look like this, graceful,
plain, in her proper place. Not like us,
with our four accented languages, with my parents
speaking Portuguese worse than the retarded kids
at school. (Mom cannot say "P." *Pah,*
pah, pah, I say. *Buh, buh, buh,* she says.)
My brother who plays soccer like a polio victim.
One look at these children, the daughters who
are not my daughters, and my heart goes out
as much to them as to forests I
have never seen, and to islands I suppose
might belong to Argentina. If
not yourself a pigeon you can encourage
flying. Yesterday we rode M.'s scooter
like cowboys into a flock of them.

Lines on the West Resist Translation

The too-cold-for-swimming Yuba carries once-snow.
Unvisited mountains, unvisited sea. We swim.

Swifter than autumn
are the river's attentions.

The locust tree seedpods
raft gamely on a journey for which they did not ask.

    *

Had their holidays been instead the Cinco
of July and Fourth of Mayo—

still would the blankets settle on the grass,
the picnic baskets disgorge

the stuff of their in-itself leisure.
It is mine to conveniently omit

all histories under this afternoon,
and keen how, how, and how again

they lived, that something of it carry
like the cormorants of my childhood

in Arromanches-sur-Mer
calling at dawn over the sea.

*

Whereof do they speak who compare
that scentless blanched flower to my homeland's cherry,
or permit the trillium the heart-glades
betrothed to the *filua*,
these unyearned for, jezebel springs?

*

The citizens go about uneasily
like a garrison loaned by a foreign court.

Stiff winds have blown them here.
It seems any wind could blow them off.

And leave the empty orange cities holding
back the dark. With the mere show

of principled tenancy I could be
the first patriot. Yet for what dowry?

The Neighbor Discusses Parkinson's

The average age of onset: fifty-eight.
The actuarial tables propose a date

but I've already beaten odds. I age
by losing the odd individual page

at a time, at intervals, all while
you fear a tragic accident. Smile,

will you. *Fatal* and *degenerative*
differ in that one will let you live

and one you leave your will. Whatever culls
the cells of the *substantia nigra* pulls

no other fast ones. I think I hear him feast,
sometimes, a pig on truffle, a picky beast

passing up the fresh cerebral bread
of *mope, resent* and *hell with this* and *dread*

left behind to clutter up my gourd.
If only Parkinson had been as bored

with motor skills. The fresh neurologist
asks how I could not have noticed

my half-mile at the pool creep up from thirty
to thirty-five and forty minutes. My birdie

turn to bogey. A stiffness in the back.
She has me in her office read the plaque

and counts my two-beat blinks. To test my balance
jabs my shoulder. Parkinson's talents

are improving monthly. Swallowing
takes concentration; my bowels, owing

three weeks of arrears, stage noisy filibusters.
My larynx sags and sulls and hardly musters

a wheeze to satisfy the *Think loud* signs
plastered everywhere like Valentines.

Anne put one on the mirror. Nothing to lose.
In about four years I will have to choose

a single victory over the medication:
the paralytic fetus, number one,

or, two, the flailing, spastic dyskinesia.
There you have it. Figures, facts, no drama,

my overt wish that you should sympathize,
sit in my goddamn den and subsidize

my hobby. In your heads live my travails.
If and when, for me, the carrot fails,

I have a serviceable stick to lever
my bony balking donkey forward. Whether

far or not, farther. Longer in the saddle.
You might exercise your choice of battle.

United Nations

Canada

You could belt my anthem whenever you liked,
then warm to the ensuing *souvenir*

France

I would turn my encyclopedic hand to your *gloire*

Mexico

My pageantry would not keep your *ojos* off my neighbor,

America,

the beefcake spaz

Uruguay

I would dedicate to you either my 1930 or 1950 World Cup victory

Norway

An exterior of staid social welfare programs would shroud
elements willing to lavish you with oil

Turkey

I would send a detachment of janissaries for your inspection

Kenya

I would rely on my animal nature to lure you
close enough to see my human side

Mars

The probes would feel ticklish. You would have to remind me
to uphold martial virtue

Uzbekistan

I would advertise more widely

China

I would focus on Sino-You relations

Minnesota

You would be my state bird

Russia

You could teach me not to take life so seriously

Antarctica

I would save you a slice

Micronesia

I have one thousand mildly radioactive paradises
to cycle as they bore you,
and I have maintained them
as though you dream of living among them

Carmon's
for P.

At noon the dust that flours the plate-glass windows
   makes Carmon's look deserted, and passersby
walking to the main post office seldom
   turn to see the shufflings of the waitress,
half-empty salt-and-pepper shakers upend
   and bobble, half-empty napkin dispensers present
the same white face no matter how many veils
   are torn from them. The men within pass around
one knee in jeans, an overall suspender,
   one moustache and one orange brim. Inside
a likeness of the cook casts impish glances
   on the impish, frantic cook. He grins and winks.

     "A customer made that ten years ago
       and she'll be tickled to see it there, if she
     ever comes around again. In case
       you think I haven't changed my hat since then,
     I go through two Cubs caps a season. That,"

he points his spatula outside and waves it—

     "that pile of bricks was once the J. C. Penney,
       and next to it the Sears, when both of them
     moved north of town the neighborhood went bad,
       on every corner prostitutes and dealers.
     Now, when I come to work at two,

the places are still all open, I could
stop and have a drink. The girls go by me
in their cocktail dresses, I go to make
the sausage and the biscuits. The owner, the owner
wouldn't budge until the doctor gave her
six weeks to live, and then she let it go,
but damned if she isn't still alive,
the biddy, meaner than a snake, meaner
than cancer. She still comes in here sometimes."

His rolling eyes encircle the decor,
carom boards and cheery forties Coke ads,
group portraits of dead football teams, a rusting
spokeshave listing on a nail. As if
a bunch of soldiers waiting out a shelling
the dolmen-men sit quietly and eat,
or not, or press up to an ear a radio
that annotates the soybean yields in China,
the Exchange's fluctuating quotes
on pork bellies and ethanol. The rains
in Argentina fall in Argentina,
mainly on the pampas, and not here,
in actuality that stretches not
all the way to Argentina, and offers
no direction in which it is not.
When the sun is up, it's up, and when it's down
it's down, and when it's only halfway up
there is a minute you can see the landscape
less its nakedness, pews of windbreaks
and high-tension power line extending
to one-quarter its diameter,
shards of standing water still as ice,
or ice. The field that three-foot balsams raster

abuts the road that no one seems to use,
which leads to silos bristling or hollow
  with the take of acreage left slovenly
and fallow, or just furrowed, or faintly
  green as though with algae or with mildew,
or so high the elephants must rear to make
  their way across. The underused equipment
gathers in its lots, hydraulic shit-churns
  and ass-kickers, luck-sumps and roto-scythes,
and no one is fornicating underneath
  the Dutch-bonnet barn roofs. Everywhere is something
almost useful. The farmers shuffle in
  to Carmon's, not running down their primes so much
as husbanding that stub of time between them
  and decrepitude, and are not like
the businessman who fidgets with a phone
  and takeout coffee cup, not like the tags
that crowd the freight cars from the South Side yards,
  the sumptuous and lapidary fonts
traversing their gazes like a news crawler
  in Arabic. Bless the sons of a bitch,
who are ill at ease most every other
  place you could call public, toting brand-new
luggage at the airport in their lime-white
  sneakers, or eating gelato, or populating
the middles of the service industry
  with unhastenable competence.

"Here," he says, and takes down off a shelf
  an album page, with one of him and "Larry"
front and center, posed in their tuxedos
  before a handsome stone municipal facade
in Ottawa, a cannon guarding them

on either side. His second favorite is of
snowflakes like silver-dollar pancakes falling
before the refurbed yellow Cape Cod saltbox
Larry is the gawky, wire-rimmed
benignant spirit of, taken five blocks
from the restaurant, perhaps at two.

III

On Janis Joplin and William Bennett's Blind Date, 1969

Hubba hubba. Of all adhesives
what but boy-girl glue could stand a chance, for
from the corner to my left
slouches the Dionysiac Texan,
guitar pick in one hand, paperback Upanishads in her other;
in *Revolución!* a solid war cry.
Has moves. Is what they call a dreamer.
And *from the corner to my right*
swaggers the Apollonian Brooklynite,
square as a squash court. Clean living,
and the kid's got credentials,

but can he stand up to flower power?
History has to be on someone's side. . . .
The smells of grilling tofu and bratwurst
waft over the picnic blanket
where the lovebirds worry their beers.
Her: a practiced antsiness come of long acquaintance
with the Eisenhower Interstate Highway System.
Him: in his head rifling a file cabinet for the
Things I Have Done Outside the Library folder.
Will his frat-boy electric guitar antics
seem, to her, parodic? flattering? desperate?

And which of these would he call
her hazy 101 recollections of Kant?

Does she really wish she were a graduate student
instead of a rock star?
Is there an undercurrent of ideological fetishism?
He brushes a mosquito from her ear.
She mistakes it for a caress
and they stare at each other, for one moment
in all eternity, moony-eyed. Just then

the host of the bourgeois appears
over the crest of the hill behind him.
Charm-school teachers wave rakes and snow shovels,
barbers snip at the air, and pig-pink oilmen
ride Cadillacs with prow-mounted longhorns.
Far out; behind her the subversives commit,
wiring their wah-wah pedals to bricks of plastique
and stacking speakers in three-high embrasures
atop the arrayed microbuses. O

unconsummated rift! By what compromising hybridizing
has the 3:2 underdog of general conformity
got the better of you? For lo,
when the tear gas clears, this chaste couple's
schizoid offspring have overrun the land like another –ism;
the drums in the junior partner's basement thwack
with abandon, abandon, abandon,
and guess who whispers
in the golfer's headphones.

Miss Lucy, *cont'd*

(Miss Lucy had a steamboat . . .)

. . . the d-a-r-k dark-dark-dark-

ness falls upon us,
and old age closes in;
luckily the children
make the same mistakes —again-

st the clock we're working,
with one foot in the fire,
one hand on the ladder
as it comes down to the —why

her mother hates me,
I guess I'll never know.
I've never even met her.
She insists on being —so-

cialism bites it,
leastways à la Marx—
just ask the homeless people
camping in the public —par-

don me that cheap shot.
I'll happily retract.
My knuckles are already
very red from being —rapt

before the statue,
the aesthete thinks of art,
the engineer its tonnage,
mayor hiding naughty —par-

ticularly nauseous,
replete with mental plaque,
the author's self-indulgence
took this critic quite a—back

in the Mesozoic,
there were no people yet.
Not much to say about it,
it just kind of came and —when

I am dictator,
I shall dictate the style:
goatees and Nehru jackets
all across my desert —I'll

do all the driving
if you buy half the gas—
I've got to get to Moosejaw
and I've got to get there —fast-

idious was the teacher,
solemn was the priest,
furious was my father
when they saw I got three —cease

your senseless prattle,
you vile, unwholesome cur,
or I'll have your carcass keel-hauled
and then skinned to keep its —for-

tune favors he who
has his back against the wall:
he has something to lean on
and a way in which to —fol-

lowing this program,
we'll have an interview
with astronaut and author
millionaire mother of —too

much salt will kill you,
like alcohol and stress,
the cigarettes and me if
you keep shouting at the —ref-

ugees run hither,
and refugees run yon,
like Lucy kicked the anthill
that she had been sitting —on-

cologists are lucky:
the salary is high,
they get to square their shoulders,
look the devil in the —i-

cicles are forming
underneath the eaves.
Three months ago or hence I
would have counted all the —leaves

in twenty minutes.
The choice is getting stark.
Miss Lucy's getting anxious
and outside it's getting dark.

Horace: Ode I, 37

Wine be drunk, then, and feet be tapped.
You shall be on your couches apt,
   Before long, to rank it
   Martian among banquets.

Good Caecuban lay cellar-bound
While that queen's mind grew more unsound
   With each conspiracy
   Against our primacy.

She deemed no counsel outrageous
That issued from her contagious
   Entourage of geldings.
   But Caesar, hard-wielding

Every oar, burned her ships to ash
And dared to call that boldness rash
   She got with narcotic
   Draughts of Mareotic;

Hawk-like after the dove he dived,
Hunter bent on the smaller-lived:
   Swift hare, this *femme fatale*,
   Snared in the snow withal

Had she not steered herself to doom.
It would have been, to flee for whom
   She paid for safe exile
   In no measure virile.

Serene before her fallen court,
Snake-clasped, she did not avert
   Hard death, but raised in toast
   The venom like a boast,

So refusing the passage back,
Where, she knew, there would be no lack
   Of those who would have blessed
   Cleopatra's conquest.

A Change of Season

All things not happening at once,
clouds came out of the east one day and warred
with callousness and frost for room in the heart.
Their terraces tendered blank invitations.
Their spires and escarpments filled
with limelight and helium.
        A thunderclap ruptured my dream of someone's
sobbing cheek between my shoulder blades.
The pad of her left pinky touched my navel, that of her
left thumb the base of my sternum, and that of her right
middle finger my left nipple.
I had been turning
Dying thunder is the sound of yolk in the dirt.
Five one-thousand before that, a bolt
had made its enraged moth-way across the front
and strobed the north-facing rooms as if they had been
six pages of a flip book.
I sat awhile in a chair.
With attention I could see the individual strokes
embark, propagate, and arrive.
It seemed like a late date for this effect
to be new to me, but I could not remember having seen it.
On the prairie a cowbird flew alone,
and the listless matted grasses brimmed like filthy carpet
with the dander of husks and castoffs.
A fawn made its way steadily and as though a carp
behind and beside its mother's head.

The bronze of the woman-statue grew greener.
The malformed samara of a maple fluttered to earth.
When I lifted the lid off the drum, a sprinkling of pollen lay
on the surface of the water, and left a taste something
like sage, very faint, on the roof of the mouth.
Teetering and half-wild before lightning and lengthening days,
I stalled, itched, scowled, and fidgeted,
did not cook, did not care for my tools or sweep.
The neighbor swore a certain tree had leafed last year in a lighter
                                                              green.

Reception seemed to be better than it had been when
the sky was mealy and ice a stony persistent mildew.
A new combine jounced west in traffic.
Two once-in-ten-years letters arrived,
a day apart, muled over the switchbacks and passes between then
                                                        and now.
On my palm the frog turned from muck-green to tawny and
                                              orange-speckled.
There are storms with no outward appearance of storminess and
                                                              one
has to ride them out, and I was aware one afternoon of
emerging into not-feeling-sick, alertness, felt
no need to account for time, which served appearances, or
                                          disappearances,
or allowed changes-in-place.
I did not mind the eucalyptus and grevillea feathering the valley,
although they were planted because they grow quickly and are
                                                          useful,
making the landscape lie at one remove from intention
like the meadows upstream of a beaver dam.
The pleasure-seeking devil in me
availed himself of the general vigor but seemed
rival to be faced rather than force of nature to flee.

It would not be necessary to withdraw.
They replaced the insulators on one of the substations, but not
                                                          on the other.
A half-brother I did not know I had appeared
with many heirs to the family name. Unburdened,
I lavished on my nephews napoleons, hamsters, and squirt guns.
For a week I filled in running the cable ferry. There was talk
among the commuters of building a bridge,
talk neither excited nor regretful.
Over coffee with a guest, I found that I remembered both
the potentate's visit, and every flood particularly.
Smelling smoke I rushed outside at night, my chin up in the dry
                                                          air
and my toes squelching in the cold grass.
When the glasses were raised I knew a toast, and when
my friends were married I blessed them unmemorably but off
                                                          the cuff.
The rebuilding of the arsoned concession stand had reached its
                                                third course of cinderblock.
My cash sat balled in a clean sock,
but neither money nor the decay of my body held any interest.
I caterwauled as I dragged my garbage cans to the curb.
In my childhood there had been an old man living in a clearing in
                                                          the woods,
and at twilight there the muntins' shadows
lay on the grass in sashes of pure slide-white.
I saw how I might occupy his house.
The season's traminette was said to be miraculous.
Air traffic doubled. Angry on the bank,
two of a bird I didn't know, and then a spooked heron
up and flapping downriver like an old man caught with his pants
                                                          down,
and then a redtail on a great circle.

The surface of the sunning turtle stretched as though
fashioned out of balloons by the magician at the petting zoo.
Fat silverfish glittered and preened in the sump.
The fastballs of the kids at the park had acquired zing.
Smells circulated of charcoal, roasting fish, manure, lilac, and
                                        superheated garbage.
The rivers roiled and were turbid but without froth.
When the creek is dry, I rebuke myself for forgetting to praise it
                                        when
just normally full, but I noticed then it was normally full.
There were relatively few dandelions, but bluebells, a yellow
                                        number
appearing in cauliflower-like bunches and smelling, though not
                                        sweet, of honey,
and a low weed with blossoms the size of quarters, with four
                                        petals,
two purple ones nearer the ground and two upper white ones.
A clear plastic bag went sailing by a hundred feet off the ground
without the slightest variation in speed or heading, a passing
piece of jetsam on a flat sea.
The sidewalks had a reddish tint, as if of fired clay,
and were clean-cracked, as though scored with a brickset.
Culottes were in and Capri pants out.
The wind that had made everyone edgy and irritable
then softened us. The lights were green or almost green,
cheers had gone up, the blackbird had puffed his chest
or was about to, the emergent leaves of the cottonwood
luffed and flapped like flypapered monarchs, without regard for
                                        each other
but with only collective effect.
There was someone in the town with whose
breathing you were falling in or out of sync.
In the field,

a flattened area like a crop circle, and three bare dirt patches
the size of bicycle wheels, making a triangle ten feet on a side.
What seam could all of it have burst along, given that it
did not
along the blue and white and yellow of heaven
and the green and brown and black of earth?
The haze clearing, from the rise I could see
the fantastic trench systems of the opposing parishes:
the one where every rose is cast in bronze,
the one where change labors inventively forever, as if cursed.

Tenth Flight

i.m. Challenger

Floridian icicles perch on the gantry.
Awaiting warmer weather, scrub
The mission hindsight warns us of?
Liftoff is rather tee minus seventy.

Without effect, for the seven sent,
We pull as hard as the several gees
The ground exacts from its escapees.
Is the pact with hydrogen not lent

Sobriety by the wishers-well?
Too-casual pluck, flight engineers'
Calm competence arouse the fears
Their very presence aims to quell—

Downrange the booster contrails tangle
That were to be the ascent's assistants.
They fall away in the middle distance.
By some other camera angle

Their escort takes its normal course:
The hula-hoop orbits never shrink
To the O-ring dunked in Feynman's drink;
Our envoys come off the tarmac hoarse

With rehearsal of their finest yarn . . .
Manta-colored, upside-down-flying omnibus:
It's not a shuttle that doesn't come back to us.
Your albatross siblings on loan from harm

Depend from the federal budget's neck,
A thick-skinned but shorthanded argosy
Steered by half-assed electronic democracy
Across the night sky. If we check,

Or not, for Canaveral's kites,
We know their curiosities
Ooze from a spring like gravity's,
And risk will come of oversights.

J. Trades in Futures

When Joseph understood the minute,
he had begun a dangerous habit
of not settling for its innate
dialect and weather. To contain it

he graduated to the hour—
ate more slowly, and left to flower
decisions he would have made cower
into yes-or-no without the power

there in patience—but could only stay
focused on what he'd given away
to get this far. Why not the day?
The evenings and afternoons anyway

pay out, endorsing whatever chic
there is in turning the other cheek
or living to fight again. And if the meek
inherit an earth made in a week,

one could hold it at least that dear
and hope to find, within the year,
room enough to misplace the fear
a dozen months will disappear.

Sketches of J.

What Joseph sees and Joseph thinks
   alternately propose their ways
   to tell apart the tones the town
   will take with him, the demi-frown
   the nurse and teller make, that says
   nothing, really, to his face.
   All of it is what it is,
   or else it is a constant quiz
   on everything that is the case.
   Should he dive, or should he swim?
   The thing he never gets across
   may prove to be his deepest loss.
   The ripples and the point of him
separate the more he sinks.

What Joseph has and Joseph wants
   tease each other, all-out fight,
   or circle warily, too proud
   to admit defeat aloud.
   He tells fame go fly a kite
   one minute, begs it back the next.
   His civic involvement could be deeper.
   Tickets to Europe were somehow cheaper.
   The unregenerate dipshit sex
   will not stay in its corner. Hell
   with money, power, status, vengeance;
   but no, hell with their complements.

The brushings-off and wishings-well
lie far apart and close at once.

What Joseph does and Joseph dreams
    have not betrayed each other yet.
    Sometimes a movement of the head
    might indicate the boundaries bled,
    a small but unacknowledged debt
    called in by a familiar gleam
    or murmur. It is getting harder
    to keep up the charade of ardor
    conversation asks of him.
    The scandals are deplorable
    over coffee and petits fours.
    My demographic can beat up yours.
    If he concurs or not, they still
seem to play on different teams.

What Joseph dreams and Joseph sees
    subsume the phantoms in the panes,
    the mockingbird whose tendered wing
    says pick a card, pick anything,
    anything. The morning feigns
    an interest in the afternoon,
    a chickadee twits like history is bunk,
    a flicker circles a poplar trunk.
    All of them will be elsewhere soon.
    The future sells its substance at
    one breath a breath, and in its essence
    the wind chime makes, of nothing, nonsense,
    and makes of nonsense orisons that
have no imperative to please.

IV

Impressions of the Tribeless

i.

Lauds for the bindi, and from the freckles
the stirring leopard-like self-satisfaction
charge the streets with cosmopolitan trappings.
We watch, and would come from the provinces
had we provinces to come from. Our hearts
will not renounce their figurative role,
so there is fondness to go around, too much
of it, and the inadvertencies
by which the city washed up on itself
have gone unsaid amid our shallow tact.
Is the heart to be made subtle, or must it
yell one harmonic yell, and in praising Venice
praise knowing-not of minaretry,
Americana, pyramidship? That city,
like this one, freehands its likeness in the water,
and that skyline not evidently given
over to commerce is beautiful, correct?
We have yet to come across a place not
so much accumulated self-portraiture,
the repository of its first excuse.
The boulevards ingrain the commonplace
of rejecting applications for being
not x enough, too y; hence the affect
of the ticket taker, the gait of those
five minutes late. All the water around
you fish. You go about your cottage industry
of making the strangeness of the stranger.

ii.

For a horizon—the kingdom we wish for for
a horizon to put it in. Through the slit
of close-penned aerogrammes in foreign hands,
hachured diagrams in the proceedings,
the short-wave radio's nighttime dictation
of counter-clockwise oceanic storms,
the widow neighbor's shaken recollections,
might enter the extravagant mystery,
in this nostalgia, not prudently kept,
for a state unhad. We do not have the license
to call our little fancies worth pursuing.
Are the hills of Connecticut burial mounds?
Do you have your own interpretation,
for children's sake, of cricket-song? And may
one eat that mushroom? We too were sodden once
with wanderlust, and continence sounded
like dumb advice. We wish those on safari
timely returns, as if the fellowships
you turned away from and intruded on
were none the better for your having gone,
and the better stagings of Arcadia
no nearer arriving for your having watched.

iii.

The guidebook is a season stale, but says,
"Sublime the clerestoried nave, deluded
its makers, who were turned loose crediting
the wishful and incredible: divinities
of a kind never found in Connecticut,
now, possibly, no longer regnant anywhere."
The park's shat-on bronzes are said to prove
"a point of different-headedness, that someone thought it

more than poor men's everlasting life
to ride a bronze horse everlastingly plinth-round."
We want to be from here, and so say, "fear
of extinction architects the commons,
as if this were a zoo of history.
The shabby, doubly suspect *chinoiseries*
are and ignore the death of that by which
the Venices they envy came to be."
The miscegenating heart we cannot fault
keeps sketching the evident, and hearing
into the Greek-to-us in the terminal
more than the chatter that we, wishful
and credent, know it to be, as we let run
that tendency to exalt beyond deserving
the odder of the last two things beheld.

Catastrophe

The reporters heard a loud report.
They marketed the crash to those
gleeful it went agley, the sort
to save face by spiting their nose.
Flocks of fish fled schools of birds.
Orange rhymed with several words.

The state refused to release a statement.
The right left the left the right
to base itself on self-abasement.
Hardened crooks went straight despite
the coppers' lead. The leaders copped.
Redemption lived on the bottle tops.

The comedians waxed tragic
but their agents seemed to lose their will.
Grinning technologists worked magic.
Leaflets on the windowsills
made a quiet compelling case
for some other time and place.

The cowboys, cowed, gave up, and then
the miners wandered in a field.
The regime abandoned its regimen.
No noun could keep our doom concealed.
When asked the wooded regions wouldn't.
The can-can dancers tried and couldn't.

Lapse of Faculty

                    pop—

Wine

The wheel, fire, leftover bowl of berries
formaldehyde

nine parts in ten. O Neolithic luck, whence
the sodden range

of two-fisted unto oenophile, solitaries unto
bons vivants

dulling edges on a stone of booze.
Already late

for even accelerants to ruin me well. The wreck
would not leave

the car-sized crater. Anesthesia raises
questions. One

awakens cottonmouthed at the midgame, the projects as
usual listing.

Women

One less hound to hound the fox miffs
the hounds, for whom

camaraderie made bearable the tyranny of the hunt.
What kind of yahoo

would roust quiescent appetites with oysters or
rhino horn

the better to enact the buffoonery of lust?
Tell the local

materies Get bent. The natives on Spitzbergen
hunt the mukmuk.

In the blinds they gesticulate, brows knit—
"*Quel dommage*,

the *Ausländers* cannot be here to taste such
delectable meat."

Song

The string section twiddles its knobs.
The event enraptures

whoever shelled out for tickets, reflecting as it does
our enlarged
capacity for something. It would be a terrible
movie. The wind

does that to bottle mouths. Those look like washtubs.
All the pomp

is not a cover-up! Felt must line the cases,
the makeup appear

as such at a distance, the bowtie sit
off-kilter on

the pianist's neck. As they intended the Argus
nods in its chairs.

Cliché Parade

The autumn brought its rust and fire.
  The town lay under a blanket of snow.
The spring returned with the entire
  Rigmarole of reap and sow.

Deep in summer the dog-like days
  Passed like ships in the summer night
Bobbing at the quiet quays
  While customs clears their loads of shite.

Parade day loomed and then arrived.
  We dressed to the nines and ate like pigs
From concessionaires who shucked and jived
  At rowdy Ghibellines and Whigs.

For a moment, it was going to happen—
  All would shed their second skins
And join in an abandoned lapping
  Of the cream-filled center at the heart of things—

Indeed on every emerald lawn
  Like leaping lords there jigged and twirled
Until the rosy-fingered dawn
  A sense that love would save the world.

Clutch

Something like a clutch, the two of us
communicate the will to one another
to move, and as one turns the other must,
in contact with his mate, turn with her,
unless the pedal disengages them
and leaves them both to whine alone in air
without a way to know the other's aim
or use their specious freedom from the pair.

If you protest my model of us makes
one the driving, one the driven, giving
one pride of place, recall life engine-brakes
as often as it climbs, and has us revving
loudest in our worst deceleration,
when on the half that had been blithe about us
is borne a little care with each gyration
to moderate our tumbling apparatus.

So they function best who come to grips,
and travel farthest fastest who beware
the mismatch of intention in the slips
that leave their coupling that much worse for wear;
let us therefore use our hard-won touch
to ride but not to ride it, me and you
pressing close together inasmuch
as is in us to be coming through.

Janet's Cottage

i.

That visitors arrive today is good and bad.
The tulips insist too firmly on the sweetness of youth;
the flagstone on the walk has cracked, and dust
has piled on the cellar sills so deep it shows
the footprints of a mouse. One door sticks.
A drizzle feints. The slipping clutch of their jalopy
whirrs in the coomb like a domestic quarrel.
They will have passed the rapeseed not yet in bloom,
and the painting of the fields they will take away
will remind them of a place it does not say.
That is good and bad. The infant sleeps.
The boy senses something and is soothed
but not comforted. Is that the sun or moon, he asks,
pointing to the summer on the easel.
The embarrassing earnestness of a private life
stretches to the horizon. Hasn't the cart
beside the haystack, at the foot of the hill,
slept under both? Someone had better take care of it, no?
If a stray came to your door, wouldn't you show
a saucer's worth of kindness? The house's stones
gather moss. In her puttering Janet reveres
a chipped enameled teapot, a black wool sweater,
a pot of chervil. The smells of earth and turpentine
make the visitors more alert and less.
They rustle in a museum of the thorough.
Things will be back to normal tomorrow.

ii.

A coppice of bottles rises from the mantel,
no two of them alike. They flare flat-bottomed
or teeter on their rounded ends and glint
in blue and all the colors of the beech. They catch
the fire- and the day-light and pass it among themselves,
a market of willowy and skittish spirits, baskets
of tinkling snakes, dried and brittle sacs
of beached sea-creatures, candy.
It seemed as if she had, in private, charmed
ice into forgetfulness of melting,
or promised them refuge, or somehow knew
the arguments they were susceptible to,
and now, in the heat of someone's gaze, they will
twinkle and abide their keeping still.
What if we break?, they do not ask.
You shall not break, she does not answer,
nor ever spill that strange, clear distillate
we do not sip from them, although the threat of it
burnishes the reflective and transparent skin
almost not there, and yet a skeleton.
The visitors draw in the breath that blew you.
So a rummaged flask decants them of the fear
they had not noticed, and a glass's delicacy shows
each of us inadequate to the place he knows.

iii.

Janet's rusted and creaking bicycle goes rolling
down past the churchyard and past
the rapeseed and the wheat fields, and Janet hums
a tune that never goes anywhere
or repeats itself. The gray afternoon,
affixed to her spirit with a hundred strings,

leaves her, for that, uncompromising as a bird.
Her brakes mouse-squeak, and then she watches
an ochre mastiff lumber out of a hedge.
It sets itself in her path and growls.
She breathes and tucks a strand of hair
behind her ear.
The mastiff barks. If she feels fear,
it is the kind one feels alone, at home,
at eleven or at two,
unsure suddenly that one is equal
to what seemed a simple task, wherewithal gone
as utterly as time. The paintbrush is a wheelbarrow
full of lead and bricks.
A thousand acres of stationery
lie immaculate in a keepsake drawer.
The kindness of a mastiff seems
a thing she will never get round to, even as it disappears
rump-last through a gap in the hedge. She hears
nothing, and then the clucking of her gears.

iv.
Over a far down a transport drops
eight paratroops for practice, as if
a girl had plucked a dandelion gone to seed.
Neither gone to storm nor drought the day
takes its terrifying middle way,
terrifying to all but Janet, who commends
the tousling *politesse* of light and shadow, and pretends
the easel is the world and the world
the easel. Is it or is it not pretend?
The village houses, seen from the hills,
or even from the street, inch closer on such quiet days
to hamlets made for model trains

of matchboxes and of cotton wool, and of
a meticulous variety of love.
Enter from the east a model train,
as quiet as a cloud. Janet watches it
up to its soft occlusion by the houses
she is almost pleased with. How splendid they are,
she thinks. The iron, the Georgian sandstone,
the gables. A little quibbling with the oils
will make a light love-labor of their toils.
They have, already, all but captured it.

v.

Time sheets off the shingles of Janet's cottage,
though a moment of impatience pry
the mortar from between the stones
as surely as a pick. The starlings nibble
fistfuls of breadcrumbs flung on the winter ground,
and the starlings nibble on the winter stars.
For years she does not mutter, *Off with his head.*
She quenches, somehow, the foolish always-wanting,
the tantrum, the listlessness and the burgeoning list,
the wail, the wrenching and the brittleness, the speculation
at the till, the cruel intimations
in the saved letter, the frayed silk of her change purse,
the expectations and the running toilet,
the endless tergiversations and the will
choking itself on the end of its chain.
How did she build her cottage with scraps at hand
to weather the thousand entropies of privacy?
The paintings hang on its inside walls, delible
shadows, frail as paper, frail as glass
through which my vermilion fire axes pass.
More noise!—and a lonely cottage will seem the less

the way one should have proceeded, and ignored
to acquire tastes for contest and reward.
Spur the needs of the body, prod ambition,
pound the fist at God's failure or man's to see
men's will or God's made evident through me.
Let in by the window imps of politics and sex
to paste up willy-nilly their unrolled verdicts—
"precious," "twee," and "quaint." —But Janet,
Janet goes riding her bicycle behind
the windbreak trees she plants within one's mind,
her attention catching all of that whose lack
has made of life an arithmetic of the shallow
and coarsened for good the matter of her praise.
Say at least no corner of the heart can hate her
long insistence that the small is greater,
if warmed beside an image of her blaze.

More Tales of Clumsy

after Gjertrud Schnackenberg

I

In purple scarf and aviator goggles,
Flailing in his mittens at the toggles,
Clumsy in the Sopwith Camel's rear
Lets fly a bluish torrent of "oh dear"
And "goodness gracious." No-No, in the front,
Wrenches the stick and pulls another stunt,

A triple-corkscrew-mega-loop-de-loop
Maraschino-cherried with a whoop.
Then he veers into a paper cloud
And Clumsy comes out grasping at the shroud
Flapping around the head he cannot reach.
There seems to be no No-No to beseech.

"What shall I do?" cries Clumsy, "I can't see!"
"Open your eyes," says No-No, and indeed
The veil has lifted! Clumsy takes a peek,
Beholds the yawning air, and with an *eek*
He shuts his eyes again. Behind his lids
Fall multitudes of yellow Perseids

Above a ballroom papered with the wrappers
Of all the years' discarded Christmas crackers,

And Noah's animals sip chocolate malts
And braid their manes, or mill around, or waltz.
A cello-playing mandrill in a mask
Absorbs himself completely in his task
Until, that is, No-No cuts the engine.

It sputters, coughs, its statement turns to question
And Clumsy has no answer but a wail.
No-No passes him a bucket. "Bail!"
He shouts, and frantically they scoop the space
Between their legs and fling it aft apace.

But Clumsy sees the ground is getting larger.
"Perhaps another tactic is in order,"
Says No-No, and climbs out on the wing preparing
To parachute to safety, thereby scaring
The stuffing out of Clumsy. "Count to ten,"
No-No, with a wink, advises, "then

"Pull the cord!"—and flops a belly-flop
Into the blue. A limpid paisley drop
Adorns poor Clumsy's eye, as he, alone,
Stands up and finds a courage of his own
Alas has come too early and too late.
Plummeting Clumsy cannot count past eight.

2

A sun with eyes closed in beneficence
With thin-lipped hint of smile extends
Eight rays, as if waving the four winds' socks
And two and four and eight and ten o'clock's.

A parched and drooping Clumsy mops his forehead.
He eyes a longhorn skull and waxes morbid.

But there—how could he have missed it?—within
The beaverboard and corrugated tin
Of a lemonade stand No-No sits
And indolently humming picks his nits.
"Lemonade—50,000,000 cents"
In lettering progressively more dense

Fills an orange magic-markered sign.
Clumsy sounds it out and gets in line.
"Sir," he whimpers, "is there, today, perhaps,
a discount?" "Discount? I discount your lapse
Of judgment, my dear Clumsy! My lemons
Grew in an orchard guarded by such demons

"As only by a nullity of virtue
May be persuaded not to try to hurt you.
I fetch my water from a crooked spring
Whose waters flow uphill, requiring
Much descent to get them at their source.
Then there is the sugar—the cane of course

"Cut with butter knives by spastic orphans
Who stuff their pillows with the unused portions."
The tip of Clumsy's tongue escapes his lips
As Clumsy, swayed, wiggles his fingertips
And darts a hand behind an outsized ear.
It comes back with a yellow metal bar

Which No-No hastily accepts, and bites.
He snaps. Four orderlies in spotless whites

Enter holding up a palanquin
On which a cushion of plush leopard skin
Bears an oblong polished silver platter
On which there stand two tumblers and decanter.

"To your good health," says No-No, hoisting
An empty glass to Clumsy who, moistening
His dusty lips, prepares at last to drink;
Mid-gulp his second thoughts already think
That something in the recipe is faulty—
The lemonade is warm and somewhat salty.

To England

To islands and the elements in all their desperation.
To lowlands giving on sea-riddled shingles.
There is no knowledge in the world for the rain to draw its
                                            curtains on.
To ancientness, to caprice, to that seething past
of no foregone conclusions, after which the one eventuality
will be a miracle. To greening and to bloodying.
To the ascendance of the ascendant.
To the Jutes, to Angles and the Saxon knife-bearers
at loggerheads, to the only land there is to dispute,
to the embroidered traceries of history
where all presence wants its mandate.
Hundred-hand horses chalked on the hillsides
graze the sparse seasons, standing invisible in the snow,
standing stark in the autumns, no giant come yet
to break them. And sheepdogs at their long-bred artistry
jostle the flocks in the meadows.
To the gauge of the yarn. To the teeth on the handsaws.
To the sizes of the dowries and the direction of the transaction.
To temper, appetite, and taste.
To apparent understanding.
As if humanity were celestial, the unfolding of events
need not suffer anyone to make sense of it.
To canals and river traffic, to wherries, lighters,
to brigs, to sea. To dreadnoughts, capital,
the dot-dot-dash of the nation's bidding, to coal soot
camouflaging the moths on the tree trunks.

A Cornish miner upturns his blackened face in the candlelight
and unwraps a pasty. The candle becomes carbide, Cornwall
                              becomes California,
the carbide becomes an electric lamp, the pasty becomes a pasty.
To Quakers in the Delaware Valley. To Virginian Cavaliers,
and East Anglians in New Haven who would hang a boy for
                              wanking.
To the New: York, Hampshire, Jersey, London, England.
The bridge is still falling down on playgrounds in Hawaii.
The children are still pocketing charms.
Ashes, ashes. To customs' stunning desertion of their authors.
Inheritance is burrs clinging to one's clothes
in the temperate woods of North America.
The European beech on the Lexington Green bears upward on
                              its purple boughs
the carved pairings of a summer day
in alphabet-juju cribbed from the Romans. I in my jotting ape
the apers of an out-of-favor scribe posted among the Britons.
I in my utterance am your interpreter posted
to an inconsequential province like Connecticut.
To the Concord Minuteman at the Old North Bridge,
never again to put down the plough or musket,
prepared for something's sake to turn against his own,
my noble savage, my dying Gaul,
steady in his embrace of treason.
In Valley Forge hang the smells of typhus,
dysentery, and fried dough. At Amritsar the rounds pierced
four people at a time, like tines in a jar of olives.
To these places, too, if
I did not think I hoisted you with your own petard,
if my occluded sympathies could tell the fluttering pigeon
in the claws of the hawk on the neighbor's porch
from a stillbirth in Australia.

80

To the scholarship you gave my mischievous mother,
who skipped home past the rubber trees with the accents
of the Irish nuns in her head,
and called a macaque a nincompoop.
To either tear from one's self all
the sordid alliances of earth,
of that post-Babel scrum I wanted no part of,
to burn away the qualities I would have liked to call my own,
or my gentle father's, or my gentle grandfather's,
or my town's, or the race's,
and not England's. Or to master them,
and not find them wanting, and run the mind's trembling hand
over that seething past having one,
miraculous eventuality, and know at every juncture what I felt:
hide, hair, grass, joinery, beech bark, coin, the page, lace,
ivory, gunwales, pudding, mortar, glass. To neither one,
to the impossibility of both, a Bronx cheer,
sparklers, a bottle of root beer in each hand, to England, *Salut*.

Utopia Sketched

The softball teams waved their counties' flags
in the warmest of the several seasons.

Patterns in the rainfall have so far confounded the almanacs.

Mongolia-shaped. One day across east-west.
But it is hard to make connections to the outlying settlements.

In guiding orchid hunters up the gorge,
our services are deemed necessary.

The linguists prowl the mountains for lost dialects.

A women's adage:
As alarm clocks on nightstands, so a man in the fields.

A variety of birds; or fish.

Decorum demanded that pianists not play their own work.

Liongo replied from across the fire,
"I have no need of faith, unless by this you mean
that which makes the spear a kind of arm,
its point willed here or there without deliberation."
Anu giggled.

The passages from Provincius lie on the tips of
                                        schoolchildren's tongues
of their own power. The teachers nevertheless make a to-do
of their memorization.
A few of the older have been abroad.
The auditoriums hush as they convene in panels.

A men's adage:
Somewhere there is a woman who doesn't care about this.

If birds, not on the migration routes.

Visiting explorers bed down in the outbuildings.
Their novelties are fobbed off on the children.

There exists a set of pronouns specifically for couples:
"How are *you-two*?"
"Fine—*we-two* finally got out to the islands this year."

At the end of the dry season we turn out in miles-long crescents
to set fire to the veldt.

Polled in the street, they respond,
"Mind the stool you're sitting on.
All else is epiphenomenon."

The masts of ships are last to vanish,
which we believe we have interpreted correctly.

The foundations at the site are almost clear.
Implements like those employed in the east have surfaced.
The steles dutifully recorded the river levels,
except for lapses in the *C* and *D* dynasties.

If fish, consider the cichlid,
one species per cove.
A children's song:
"Triangular hens lay spherical eggs.
The faster you run, the longer your legs.
Laugh from otter beats smile from fish.
Think hard before making your second wish."

Rain pools in depressions worn in the steps of the capital.

Conquerors from the northwest sowed features among us
neither desirable nor un-: cleft chins, strange bowlines on the
                                                    hawsers,
double-entry bookkeeping.

Notes

"Safiya's Recife Diary": "Magic carpet" is an allusion to "Operation Magic Carpet" of 1949-50, in which almost all of the Yemenite Jewry was airlifted to Israel. See Reuben Ahroni's *Yemenite Jewry: Origins, Culture, and Literature* (Indiana University Press, 1986) or S. D. Gotein's *From the Land of Sheba* (Shocken Books, 1973).

"Tenth Flight": This poem's title is taken from the *Challenger*'s tenth flight, on 28 January 1986. "Electronic democracy" refers to the computers available at the time the shuttle was designed, which were so unreliable that four of them were installed. Navigation problems were fed to all four simultaneously and the majority opinion taken.

D. H. Tracy's poems, translations, essays, and reviews have appeared in *American Poetry Review*, *Poetry*, *The New York Times Book Review*, *Literary Imagination*, *The Iowa Review*, *TriQuarterly*, *Prairie Schooner*, and *Contemporary Poetry Review*. He has served as editor of the Poetry Foundations's online archive.